BYGONE ·N·O·R·W·I·C·H·

— AN —
·A TO Z·

— by —

Dean Parkin

with

C. R. Temple

RUSHMERE PUBLISHING

Picture Credits

Norwich Library 4, 6, 25, 31, 34, 35, 42, 43, 47; Norwich Union 7, 38, 39, 41, 46; Clifford Temple 5, 8, 9, 12, 13, 14, 15, 17, 18, 19, 20, 22, 23, 24, 26, 27, 29, 30, 32, 33, 36, 40, 44, 45, 48; Simon Baker 16, 21.

First Published 1990 by Rushmere Publishing
32 Rushmere Road, Carlton Colville, Lowestoft, Suffolk

Typeset by Anglia Repro Services
133 South Quay, Great Yarmouth, Norfolk

Printed in England by Waveney Print
Gosford Road, Beccles, Suffolk

ISBN 1 872992 00 5

Acknowledgements

I would like to thank the many people who have helped with information and advice during the production of this book. My especial thanks are due to the staff of the Norwich and Lowestoft Libraries; James Duffell, Public Relations, Norwich Union; Peter Box for his continuing help and encouragement and Simon Baker for his time and assistance.

I would also like to express my appreciation to David and Christine Johnson, who have been a constant source of help, hope and guidance and initially gave me the chance to do something of which I would otherwise never have even dreamed.

Finally a special word of thanks must go to Clifford Temple of Norwich, who has so kindly allowed me a selection of photographs from his comprehensive collection and whose personal knowledge going back over many years has been invaluable.

BYGONE NORWICH

– AN A TO Z –

A – Around the Market

B – Blitz

C – Castle and Cathedral

D – Diary

E – Entertainment

F – Norwich Fair

G – Guildhall

H – Historic Houses

I – In Retrospect

J – Just a Memory

K – The King's Coronation

L – Lord Mayor's Coach

M – Markets

N – Norwich Union

O – On the Ball City!

P – Peter Mancroft

Q – Quayside

R – Remember?

S – Shopping

T – Trams

U – Unforgettable?

V – Vintage Norwich

W – Westlegate

X, Y, Z – Three Views of Bygone Norwich

A

Around the Market

Nos. 34 and 35 the Market Place, circa 1935. Fulcher's Dining ▶ Rooms is now a clothes shop though the *Sir Garnet Wolseley* public house, on the right of the photograph can still be found there.

Previously a butchers shop, the public house was named after a notorious British soldier of the nineteenth century, who fought in such battles as the Burmese War in 1852–53, where he was badly wounded; in the Crimea, where he lost an eye and the Chinese War in 1860. During his life he served as a Major-General, a Viscount, a Field Marshall and Commander-in-Chief of an expedition to Egypt in 1882. By then he was a national figure and it seems likely that it was around this time that the public house was opened and given his name.

A photograph taken during the Silver Jubilee celebrations of King ▶▶ George V in 1935. In front of the Guildhall (the building on the left), is the War Memorial which was moved to a site in the Ornamental Gardens in front of the City Hall in 1938. Chamberlin's was founded in 1815 and was a haberdashery and drapery business. In 1898 the store had to be rebuilt after it was ravaged by fire. The site is now occupied by Tesco's Supermarket.

B

Looking up Rampant Horse Street, from St. Stephen's Street in the late 1920s. On the left is Buntings, which is currently occupied by Marks and Spencer. All the property on the right was destroyed during bombing in World War Two.

Photograph showing all that was left of Rampant Horse Street a year after the German raid in 1942 which also damaged buildings in Brigg Street, Orford Place and Red Lion Street and which were later demolished as a result.

On the right of the photograph stands a large static water tank, erected for wartime purposes. Many thought that it would later be ideal for a municipal swimming bath, but at the end of the War an alternative site was found and the tank emptied and used as a car park. Later a new building was built on the site, which is presently occupied by Debenhams.

By the end of the Second World War it was estimated that Norwich had had more than 1,450 bomb alerts and 670 high explosives and 25,000 incendiaries dropped on it, killing 350 people and wounding 1,100. Around 30,000 houses had been damaged, 2,000 of which were beyond repair.

C

Castle and Cathedral

The early development of the City of Norwich owes a lot to the Norman Conquest and here we see three of the legacies of that period, the Market, the Castle and on the far left, the Cathedral.

The present Norwich Castle was established around 1075 by the Normans to help maintain law and order in their new kingdom. They forced the defeated Saxons to dig the moat and raise a forty foot high mound. The Castle never played an important role in the defence of the City, although in the early years of the reign of Henry III (1216–1272) it was actually captured by King Louis of France, who was later defeated at Lincoln. With the erection of the City Wall between 1294 and 1340 its role became even less significant.

By 1220 part of the Castle had become the residence of the Sheriff of Norfolk whilst the other part became the County Gaol. In 1792 some new additions were made to the Castle's prison facilities, but by 1814 these had to be demolished to make way for bigger buildings. By this time the Castle had fallen into a state of disrepair with the crumbling walls freely plundered for building materials by the people of Norwich! Restoration was urgently needed and the task was assigned to Anthony Sahin who between 1834 and 1839 restored the Castle to its former glory.

In 1887 the Corporation bought the Castle and began to convert it to its present use as a museum, and it was opened on the 23rd October 1894 by the Duke and Duchess of York (who later became King George V and Queen Mary).

Norwich Cathedral, March 31st, 1953. The Union Jack is flying at half-mast following the death of Queen Mary.

After William the Conqueror replaced the Saxon Bishop with Herfast, a man of Norman origin, in 1094, he transferred the See of East Anglia from Thetford to Norwich so that the Castle would be able to offer protection in the event of any trouble. It was under the command of Herbert de Losinga, Herfast's successor, that the construction of a new cathedral and its surrounding buildings began in 1096. The size of the operation was such that a canal was dug from Pull's Ferry to the site of the Cathedral, so that stone could be brought straight from Caen in Normandy and Barnack in Northamptonshire. When de Losinga died in 1119, the Cathedral was almost completed and he was buried in the chancel, commemorated by an effigy, which is today thought to be the oldest of its kind in England.

Norwich Cathedral is 416 feet long and of cruciform design and as well as having the largest cloisters in Britain it also has one of the tallest spires, which at 315 feet, is second only to Salisbury Cathedral. It was built in 1362 after the previous wooden one was destroyed in a hurricane.

Through the years the Cathedral has been ravaged with fire, pillaged during the reformation and bombed by the Germans in 1942. After the Second World War, long and extensive restoration work was carried out on the ancient building, and on its completion in 1975, a Service of Thanksgiving was held which was attended by the Queen.

Today the Cathedral, or to give its official title, The Church of the Holy and Undivided Trinity, is visited by thousands of people each year and is one of the few remaining examples of Norman architecture.

D

Diary

A.D.

446 The foundation of Norwich.

575 A Castle was built at Norwich by Uffa, King of the East Angles.

872 King Alfred improved the fortifications in Norwich.

980 Norwich was made a Borough, governed by a Sergeant.

1010 The Danes returned to England, subdued the East Angles and settled in Norwich.

1030 Norwich was a prominent fishing town.

1075 Ralph de Waiet was made the Earl of Norwich. He later rebelled against William the Conqueror, though was defeated.
The original St. Peter Mancroft Church was built by Ralph de Guader, the Earl of Norfolk.

1094 8th April, Bishop Herbert de Losinga moved the See of East Anglia from Thetford to Norwich.

1096 The first stone of the Norwich Cathedral was laid.

1119 Bishop Herbert de Losinga died while the Cathedral was in its final stages of completion.

1135 King Stephen granted Hugh Bigod the custody of the Castle.

1152 Stephen made Norwich a Corporation.

1174 Supporters of Hugh Bigod, who rebelled against Henry II, plundered and pillaged their way through the City.

1278 The Cathedral was consecrated on Advent Sunday by the Bishop, William de Middleton.

1216 King Louis of France captured Norwich Castle in his bid to conquer England, only to be defeated at Lincoln.

1266 Displaced Barons seized the Castle and plundered the City.

1294 The construction of the City Walls began.

1296 Norwich first sent representatives to Parliament.

1340 A public tournament took place at which King Edward III and Queen Phillipa were present.
The City Walls were completed.

1348 57,000 people died from the Plague in Norwich.

1362 The Cathedral's spire collapsed.

1377 The population of Norwich was 5,300.

1407 Construction began on the Guildhall.

1413 Part of the City was damaged by fire.
Guildhall was completed.

1420 Erpingham Gate, one of the entrances to the Upper Close, was built in memory of Thomas Erpingham who fought in the Battle of Agincourt in 1415, commanding the archers.

1430 The rebuilding of St. Peter Mancroft Church began.

1463 The Cathedral's roof was destroyed by fire.

1477 The Plague returned to Norwich.

1507 A fire destroyed 718 houses in the City.

1509 Fire ravaged the Cathedral's interior.

1549 Robert Kett, a tanner of Wymondham, led a peasants' revolt against the wealthy landlords, because of their enclosure of common lands. Kett's men marched to Norwich and made an encampment on Mousehold Heath. The insurrection lasted for seven weeks and was eventually crushed by an army led by the Earl of Warwick. 3,000 of the rebels were slain in battle and some were executed. Kett and his brother William were taken to London and charged 'that they did feloniously and traitorously make an insurrection and levy war against our lord the King.' Robert Kett was hanged at Norwich Castle while his brother met the same fate at Wymondham Church.

1575 Dutch immigrants settled in Norwich, manufacturing corded fabric made of silk or worsted known as bombazines.

1597 A ruling was made declaring that no-one should serve as Mayor for a second term for a period of nine years after their first appointment.

1601 29th April, the Cathedral spire was struck by lightning.

1602 Over three thousand people died in an outbreak of the Plague in the City.

1648 John Utting, the Mayor, was sent to a new post in London despite a petition being presented to him by 150 people begging him to stay. Utting was very popular with the poorer people of Norwich and as soon as he left an angry mob marched to the Committee House, where gun powder was kept, and set fire to five barrels, killing one hundred people and damaging adjacent buildings.

1650 Twenty-four people were hanged at Norwich for supporting the Stuarts attempt to regain the Crown.

1673 Snow which had lain from late February till Easter suddenly thawed and caused a great flood.

1712 An Act of Parliament was obtained for the erection of a Workhouse at Norwich.

1738 The population of Norwich was 33,000.

1758 31st January, the Grand New Opera Concert Hall was opened.

1766 The people of Norwich rioted because of a shortage of food and many buildings were damaged as a result.

1768 The Grand New Opera House was renamed the Theatre Royal.

1770 Work began on the construction of the Norfolk and Norwich Hospital facing St. Stephen's Street.

1785 Friday 23rd July, Major Money began a journey in a balloon from the City, passing over Pakefield and out to sea, where it descended, leaving the Major to struggle for four hours before being rescued!

1792 Gentlemen's Walk was paved with Scottish granite.
The demolition of the twelve City gates began. The gates, which were damaged during Kett's rebellion in 1549, were part of Norwich's fortifications. The Corporation decided to demolish them partly in the interests of hygiene but mainly because of the cost of their repair and maintenance. They were all destroyed by 1808.

1802 A new wing was added to the Norfolk and Norwich Hospital.

1825 The Theatre Royal was demolished and a new one was built on adjoining land.

1826 27th March, the new Theatre Royal was opened.

1834 Restoration work began on the Castle.

1849 7th November, a passenger train departed from the City for the first time. Its destination was Ipswich.

1854 The statue of Wellington was erected in the Market Place.

1857 The Norwich Free Library was built, believed to be the first ever purpose-built library in the country. It stood at the corner of St. Andrew Street and Duke Street.

1879 Horse-drawn buses first operated in Norwich.

1880 Mousehold Heath is given to the City by the Church, on condition that it is forever used for the recreation of the people.

1882 The Agricultural Hall, now the premises of Anglia Television, was built.

1887 The Corporation bought the Castle and began to convert it into a Museum.

1894 23rd October. The Castle Museum was opened by the Duke and Duchess of York.

1895 A spire was added to St. Peter Mancroft Church.

1898 The first tramlines in the City were laid.
Norwich City Fire Station was opened at 12–14 Pottergate.

1900 30th July, trams came into service at Norwich after a formal opening.

1903 The Norwich Hippodrome was opened as the Grand Opera House.
Work began on the construction of the Jarrold's Store in London Street.

1907 Norwich City F.C. moved from their Newmarket Road ground to the Old Nest. The opening game at the new ground was against West Ham, with a crowd of 29,779 watching a 4–3 win by the 'Canaries'.

1911 The Lord Mayor's coach was presented to Norwich by the former Mayor, Sir Eustace Gurney.

1912 Seven inches of rainfall caused flooding in the City. Three people died.

1915 11th November, the Thatched Cinema in All Saint's Green opened. The premises had formerly been known as the Thatched Assembly Rooms.

1921 The Maddermarket Theatre was founded by Nugent Monck and the Norwich Players, who converted an old building into an Elizabethan-style theatre. Presently it is still in use.

1930 The Thatched Cinema closed.

1932 Work began on the new City Hall.

1934 22nd June, the Theatre Royal was burnt down.
Norwich City F.C. moved to Carrow Road.
Norwich City Fire Station was transferred to Bethel Street.

1935 30th September, the present Theatre Royal was opened.
10th December, Norwich's last tram ran.

1937 The statue of Wellington was moved from the Market Place to the Cathedral Close.

1938 29th October, the new City Hall was opened. It had cost £384,000 to build.

1940 9th July, Norwich suffered its first air-raid. In all there were an estimated 1,450 bomb alerts, 670 high-explosive bombs and 25,000 incendiaries dropped on the City during the course of the War.

1942 April, Norwich had its heaviest air-raid of the War causing a great loss of life and extensive damage to buildings.

1954 22nd February, the Startrite Shoe Factory was destroyed by fire.

1958 Norwich City F.C. embarked on the famous F.A. Cup run, which was to see them beat Manchester United and Tottenham, only to lose to Luton in the Semi-Finals.

1958 The Haymarket Picture House was demolished.

1960 The Cattle Market, formerly sited in what is now Anglia House, moved to Harford Bridges, opening on the 1st July.
The Norwich Hippodrome closed.

1961 Work began on widening St. Stephens Street.

1962 Urgent maintenance work was carried out on St. Peter Mancroft Church, which was in danger of collapsing.

1964 The Norwich Free Library was demolished.

1965 London Street was pedestrianised.

1966 Norwich Hippodrome was auctioned and sold, and eventually demolished.

Cavalry Barracks in Barrack Street was demolished to make way for a housing development.

1967 The Council bought the Theatre Royal.

1970 August, Garlands, a prominent local store in London Street, was destroyed by fire.

1972 Norwich City F.C. were promoted to the First Division for the first time.

1975 Restoration work on the Cathedral was completed and a Thanksgiving Service was held, which was attended by the Queen.

1977 The Boar's Head Inn became a branch of Lloyds Bank.

1980 Norwich City F.C. sell Kevin Reeves to Manchester City for a million pounds.

On the cold, wintery night of 22nd February 1954, the Norwich ▶ Startrite Shoe Factory at Charing Cross was devastated by fire, which caused thousands of pounds worth of damage. The fire took over three hours to control, and at its height thirty firemen with eight water jets bravely battled against the flames. Their job was made more difficult by the lack of space around the rear and sides of the building which meant that the fire could only be tackled from the front.

The firm's machinery and stock were completely destroyed, but within a few days the Company began making plans to re-open in adjacent premises.

A view from St. Peter Mancroft Church showing the City Hall, the Guildhall and Market Place in 1953. In the 1920s it became apparent that the Corportion had outgrown its premises near the Market Place and was in need of larger buildings. In 1926 tentative plans emerged for a new City Hall and many of these original proposals were incorporated in the final scheme.

Subsequently the old municipal buildings were demolished and larger, modern premises built on the same site. Opened in 1938, the building received acclaim for its architecture and was described by Nicholas Pevsner as 'the foremost English public building constructed between the wars'. The locals, however, called it 'the marmalade factory'!

The Norwich Hippodrome, in St. Giles Street, was originally opened as the Grand Opera House in 1903. During its lifetime it was used as an opera house, variety playhouse, music hall and cinema and during its later years became a popular theatre, before it finally closed in 1960. In January 1966 the building was auctioned and sold, and the site was subsequently redeveloped.

Today a multi-storey car park is situated where the Hippodrome once stood.

Some famous names from show business performed on the stage of the Norwich Hippodrome. In February 1954 perhaps the most popular and well known of all double-acts, Laurel and Hardy, played at the Hippodrome for a week's run, receiving £1000 for their efforts — a record fee at the time. Prices to see the show, 'Birds of a Feather', ranged from £1 for a four-seater box to 2s 6d for a seat in the stalls.

The present day Theatre Royal shortly before its refurbishment in 1990. Opened in 1935, it was built on the site of its predecessor which burnt down the previous year.

The original Theatre Royal was established in 1757 during the theatrical revival in the eighteenth century. Originally known as the 'Grand New Concert Hall', it was renamed the Theatre Royal in 1768, after an Act of Parliament for the licensing of theatres was given the 'Royal' Assent. By 1819 it became apparent that the old theatre was inadequate and in 1825 it was demolished and its successor built on an adjoining site. Costing £6,000 to build, it seated a thousand and was opened on the 27th March 1826. Unfortunately it always proved difficult to attract the top music hall acts out of the big cities to provincial theatres, though in 1904 an aspiring young Charlie Chaplin is said to have appeared at the Theatre Royal, in a production of the 'Lancashire Lad'!

On Friday the 22nd June 1934 the Theatre Royal was ravaged by fire. A new theatre promptly rose out of the ashes and was completed within fifteen months, opening on the 30th September 1935. The Second World War did at least give the theatre the chance to host the top shows which had been driven away from the Capital by heavy bombing. However Norwich too suffered its own 'blitz', in April and June 1942, when the theatre was hit by three incendiary bombs though was not seriously damaged.

In the 1950s the theatre was partly converted into a cinema due to the advent of 'Cine-Variety'. This was when the first part of the show would be a live act, such as Lonnie Donnegan, Max Bygraves or Billy Cotton, while in the second part a feature film would be shown. By the 1960s the theatre hosted one-off appearances by pop stars such as Cliff Richard, Cilla Black, Lulu, Adam Faith, Joe Brown and the 'Bruvvers', Billy Fury and Marty Wilde. Despite this the theatre was still not economically viable and in 1966 plans were put forward to convert it into a bingo hall. Thankfully this idea was vetoed by the Council which decided to buy the theatre themselves a year later for £90,000. Initially this proved to be an unsuccessful investment, until the appointment of Richard Condon as general manager, who has helped the theatre achieve national importance.

Though the theatre was closed in the summer of 1990 for refurbishment, a big top was erected at Earlham Park so that the theatre's shows could continue while the work was completed.

Cliff Richard was one of the growing number of pop stars to appear ▶ at the Theatre Royal in the 1960s. Here he is caught as he tried to slip into the back entrance of the Theatre Royal unnoticed, to avoid another chaotic reception by hundreds of adoring fans.

Stalls at the Norwich Fair in the 1950s. The Fair is of obscure origins, though it is believed that it was originally held just before Easter, at Tombland. In 1686 it was ordered by proclamation that the Fair should be held on Maundy Thursday. By the mid-nineteenth century the site of the fair was the old cattle market, where it remained until 1988 when it moved to the new cattle market in Hall Road.

Guildhall

London Street, June 1899, Howlett's Corner. An old gaslamp is on the left, while situated on the right are Rudd's and Jarrolds. In the centre is the Guildhall, looking much the same as it does today, though to its left are the old municipal offices, which were demolished in the 1930s to make way for the new City Hall.

The Guildhall was originally a small thatched building, erected as a toll house for collecting the tolls from the market stallholders during the reign of Edward III (1327–1377). It was called the 'Toll Booth' though in the latter years of Edward's reign, around the same time as an extension was added to the building, it became known as the 'Guildhall'. When Henry IV (1422–1462) granted the City a Charter for electing Mayors instead of Bailiffs, it was decided to build a new Guildhall as the old one was proving to be too small. Unfortunately the King did not give any financial support to the cause, leaving Norwich to raise its own funds. In 1407 a committee was established and among its many parochial duties was to decide how to raise money for the building of a new Guildhall. Within a year they had raised enough for work to begin, the building finally being completed in 1413.

The Guildhall no longer has a municipal purpose and is currently a Tourist Information Office.

The historic *Briton Arms* at Elm Hill, formerly an inn but now a coffee house, standing next to the original elm tree, from which the street took its name. The tree has since been removed. Opposite stands the church of St. Simon and St. Jude while at the other end of the street is the entrance to Father Ignatius' ancient monastery.

A century ago Elm Hill was derelict, but after the First World War it came into the possession of the Council which was persuaded to restore the ancient buildings to their former glory.

Prince of Wales Road. The postcard on the left shows the road around the beginning of the century, while the photograph below shows the same view in 1990.

Prince of Wales Road was built in the mid-nineteenth century, and has many fine buildings sited along its path, such as the Royal Hotel which was erected in 1896–97. On the far right of these two views is the former Agricultural Hall, which was constructed in 1882, while alongside it is the old Post Office which was originally the Crown Bank, built in 1866. These two buildings have been joined and are now the premises of Anglia Television.

21

A view of Charing Cross, taken in 1956. The premises on the left were occupied by Havers, the ironmonger; Dyer, the shoe repairer; Knowles the tobacconist; the Free Library and the Corporation baths. The library opened in 1857 and is believed to have been the first purpose-built one in the country. In 1963 a new Central Library was opened in Bethel Street by H.M. Queen Elizabeth, the same year as its predecessor was demolished — along with all the other properties on the left of the photograph — with part of the new telephone exchange built on the site.

Red Lion Street decorated to celebrate the Coronation of King George VI in 1937. One visitor complimented Norwich on its impressive street decorations, describing them as, 'The best I have seen anywhere outside London!'

Lord Mayor's Coach

Photograph showing the Lord Mayor's coach leaving the Erpingham Gate at Norwich Cathedral in 1953. The coach is used several times a year for such occasions as Lord Mayor's Day, the opening of the assizes and for various civic functions at the Cathedral. The coach was presented to the Norwich Corporation on the 11th October 1911 by the City's Lord Mayor, Sir Eustace Gurney, who had first used the coach for the visit of King George V in the previous June. After the Second World War there were fears that the use of the coach would be discontinued as no horses could be found, but in 1950, Steward and Patterson, a local brewery, came to the rescue offering to provide the coach with two Percheron horses which were normally used for hauling their drays. The custom continued until 1969 when the brewery, which had by then become part of Watney Mann, retired the horses, leaving the coach's future use in jeopardy once again. This time Watney's offered to provide two bay shires, with a coachman, whenever the coach was used. This association lasted until 1975 when Watney's, which by then had no business interests remaining in the City, announced that, because of the estimated £50,000 it cost to keep the two horses, they were forced to sell them.

More recently, since early 1985, the famous Norwich Union Greys have provided the Lord Mayor's coach with 'horsepower', keeping alive a tradition which has now almost spanned this century.

An interesting view of the Market Place in May 1854. In the centre of the market is the statue of Wellington, erected in the same year but moved to the Cathedral Close in 1937 during the redevelopment of the area. The white building on the left with the flagpole, was the Royal Hotel, formerly the site of the Angel Hotel, which was where Thomas Bignold called the meeting to establish the Fire Office, the forerunner to Norwich Union, in 1797.

It is claimed that the Saxons, after their conquest of East Anglia, were responsible for the establishment of Norwich market to enable them to sell produce from their prosperous agricultural trade. By the time the Normans invaded, the market was being held in the area of Tombland, and one of the reasons why the suspicious Normans built their military headquarters near the site of (what was later to be) Norwich Castle, is thought to be so they could keep a watchful eye on the market's tumultuous crowds.

By the fourteenth century most of the stalls had gradually moved to the site of the present day Provision Market and were selling cloth, hats, rope, soap and books, while a fish market also traded in the area. In the event of toothache sufferers sought the advice of a dentist who was also said to have plied his trade there!

In the 1930s the Market Place was refurbished as part of the plan which involved the construction of the new City Hall. The confused jumble of stalls were re-arranged into an orderly network of rows, pleasing to the eye as well as more convenient for customers. Since then the Market has changed very little, though it has had to adapt to present day needs, and today it features stalls offering services as diverse as fast food and watch repairs. Hygiene has been dramatically improved, and hot and cold water facilities are now provided, as the stall holders strive to attract customers in a highly competitive City centre.

The Cattle Market, near Prince of Wales Road, in the late 1920s. The site was a car park for many years but is currently being redeveloped.

The Cattle Market moved around the area of Tombland until the early seventeenth century when it was transferred to a site east of the Castle, with cattle pens standing at the rear of the Agricultural Hall in Prince of Wales Road. The Hall is now Anglia House, home of Anglia Television, while the land where the cattle pens stood is now a car park. As early as 1937 it was realised that the Cattle Market was causing a traffic problem, so the Markets' Committee gave serious consideration to moving it. This was the cause of much argument as to whether trade would suffer if any move was made, so it wasn't until 1960 that the plan was eventually implemented and the Cattle Market moved to Harford Bridges, a site two-and-a-half miles away from the centre of Norwich, where it remains to this day.

Photograph taken from the corner of Surrey Street and All Saints Green, showing the Norwich Union building under construction during the Company's redevelopment of the area around their Head Office in the 1950s. The origins of Norwich Union date from the late eighteenth century after Thomas Bignold realised that there was an unfilled gap in the insurance service, having tried unsuccessfully to arrange insurance protection against highwaymen for a journey from Kent to Norwich. As a result, he established the Norwich Union Fire Office in 1797 and the Life Society in 1808 with these two companies remaining separate until 1925 when they were merged into one.

The Bignold's old Georgian house in Surrey Street today stands at the centre of Norwich Union's modern office complex and is still in use as both a training facility and the group's museum. Surrey House, which was originally the headquarters of the Life Society, stands adjacent, and presently houses management offices and the boardroom. Norwich Union is now the biggest employer in the city, presently with over 5500 staff and is continually expanding.

One of the most exciting periods in Norwich City F.C.'s history was the glorious F.A. Cup run of 1958–59 when the Club, languishing in the Third Division South, battled their way to a place in the Semi-Finals against all odds. Pictured is the team that got them there: Back row, left to right; McCrohan, Thurlow, Nethercott, Butler, Ashman and Crowe: Front row, Crossan, Allcock, Bly, Hill and Brennan.

After overcoming Ilford and Swindon in the early rounds of the competition, Norwich were drawn at home to Manchester United. United were near the top of the First Division and had been F.A. Cup finalists in the previous two seasons and it came as quite a shock when Norwich won the game 3–0. In the following rounds Norwich's march to Wembley continued beating Cardiff 3–0 and First Division Tottenham 1–0 after a 1–1 draw.

In the Quarter-Finals Norwich faced Sheffield United which was fifth in the Second Division. This proved to be another close encounter which saw Norwich grab a 3–2 victory. The hero of the match was Norwich's goalkeeper Ken Nethercott who, despite dislocating his shoulder, overcame the pain to help his side secure a Semi-Final place, a match he would himself miss due to the injury.

On the 14th March, 1959, Norwich City proudly ran out alongside Luton Town in the F.A. Cup Semi-Final. The match ended in a 1–1 draw with Norwich unluckily having a goal disallowed. Though the 'Canaries' narrowly lost the replay 1–0, the story is still fondly told today, over thirty years later, about the unlikely Third Division side which should have won the F.A. Cup!

We are the champions! Norwich City F.C. are given an enthusiastic welcome by their fans outside their Carrow Road ground after having won the Second Division Championship in May 1972, gaining promotion to the First Division for the first time in their history.

The players who can be seen on the bus are Terry Anderson, Douglas Livermore, Maxi Briggs, Graham Paddon and Jimmy Bone.

P

Peter Mancroft

A view from the City Hall in July 1953, of St. Peter Mancroft Church, the largest parish church in Norwich. On the left of the photograph, behind the Church, is the new Bond's store being built. All the buildings to the right of the picture have been demolished and the site is now the Bethel Street car park.

The church is another legacy of the Norman Conquest and was built around 1075 by the Earl of Norfolk, Ralph de Guader. It is dedicated to St. Peter and St. Paul though the origins of 'Mancroft' are unclear. Two popular theories are that the church was built on land known as the *Magna Crofta* or that the name of the owner of the land was *Man, Mann, Manni* or *Manne*.

Ralph de Guader rebelled and lost against William the Conqueror, and so the church was passed to one of the King's Chaplains, Wala, who in turn gave it to the Abbey of St. Peter at Gloucester after he had joined the Benedictine monks there. For more than three hundred years the church remained under the Abbey's control and by the late fourteenth century the building had fallen into a state of disrepair. In 1388 the church passed to the local Benedictine

community, St. Mary-in-the-Fields, whose own church stood on the site now occupied by the Theatre Royal. The neglect of St. Peter Mancroft Church was such that it was decided to rebuild it rather than try to repair the decaying structure. It took forty years to raise enough funds to build the new church but finally in 1430, the first stone was laid and twenty-five years later the present day St. Peter Mancroft Church was finally completed and consecrated.

Subsequently the church has survived Henry VIII's reformation of churches, though suffered a great deal of damage during World War Two, when so many ancient examples of architecture were lost. More recently perhaps the biggest threat to its safety occurred in the early 1960s when the church was in danger of collapsing under the weight of the roof, which was causing immense strain on the ageing walls. From 1962 two years of painstaking work was carried out to save the church, with the roof being raised on jacks and the keeling walls pulled back.

Today the St. Peter Mancroft Church has an even wider ministry due to the redundancy of many of its neighbouring churches.

Two vessels, the *River Trent* of Hull and the *Formality*, unload at Norwich quayside in the early 1950s.

After the Second World War the port of Norwich declined, heavily affected by the dwindling coal industry. Despite this there was still a steady flow of traffic in the Yare in the 1970s which increased in the following decade, generated by the Broads yachts and cruisers in addition to the many 'working' vessels which still unload at Norwich.

Norwich is strategically placed at the confluence of the Rivers Yare and Wensum. The stone to build Norwich Cathedral was brought by river up to Pull's Ferry and then along a canal to the site. Up to the early fifties, coal was still being quanted up the river as in this scene on the Wensum near Bishops Bridge.

The shops and houses of Grapes Hill. In 1967/68 all of these buildings were demolished as part of a plan to ease the City's ever-increasing traffic problem.

Bushell and Co., Castle Street circa 1950. Bushells were a prominent local shop, selling goods as diverse as handbags and 'doggie requisites'. The premises have been converted into two and are now both occupied by travel agents.

A view of White Lion Street in 1908. The street is now pedestrianised though has changed very little in appearance. The shop on the left, Pooley's, is currently the premises of a travel agent, while Cozen's Hairdressing Salon is now occupied by a sandwich bar.

◀Car No. 10, on the Earlham Road route which was one of those first opened, being slowed down by a nonchalant shepherd and his herd.

There were many references to the tram causing inconveniences, such as that which occurred in the narrow part of King Street, near Rose Lane where Mr. Wiseman's butchers shop was once situated. His pony and cart would frequently obstruct the oncoming trams and so the pony was continually being moved to the other side of the street and back. Soon the animal began to acquire the habit and when he heard a tram coming he would move to the other side of the road on his own, and automatically return when it had gone!

There had been many schemes put forward for the introduction of trams since the advent of electricity in Norwich in 1881, encouraged by the City Council's preference for a privately owned tram service. However, it wasn't until the turn of the century that trams were finally introduced by the New General Traction Company which beat off competition from the British Electric Tram Company to win the right to operate a tram service in Norwich.

Before the tram lines could be laid the Council had to repair many of the old roads in the City, in addition to the widening of streets and construction of new roads. The total cost of these improvements was estimated at £100,000, with £34,000 met by the New General Traction Company.

On the 22nd June 1898 work on the tramlines finally began and by 1900 the lines in Thorpe Road, Earlham Road and Orford Place were completed, with trial runs being held on them in April of that year. On the 30th July 1900 Car No. 20 formally opened Norwich tramways by travelling on all the routes on which services commenced the same day. The tramways proved to be an instant success, with an estimated 400,000 passengers carried in the first two weeks of its opening!

In 1917 tram cars helped the war effort by carrying notices saying 'Hostile Aircraft Approaching — Take Cover', which would be displayed in the event of any impending air-raid. During these hostilities manpower was scarce, so the Tram Company employed women as conductors (though not as drivers!). Within a year of the War ending, services had returned to normal, though in the following decade the tracks began to show signs of wear. Unfortunately money was scarce and there were simply not enough funds to repair the ageing lines and in 1924 the New General Traction Company introduced motor buses on some routes and gradually replaced the trams. In 1932 the Council had the option to buy the Traction Company, but after much argument and public discussion it was decided against the idea. A year later the Traction Company, with its 44 tram cars, 33 motor buses and a parcel van, was bought by the Eastern Counties Omnibus Company.

The last tram service at Norwich ran on the 10th December 1935, carrying passengers from Newmarket Road to Cavalry Barracks. A crowd of five hundred people had gathered at the trams starting point at Orford Place, and there was quite a scramble to board it! The passengers sang *Auld Lang Syne* with cheering crowds lining the pavements along the route. It was only on the return journey when the passengers got fewer, that the conductor, who had been penned in on the top deck of the crowded tram, was able to collect the fares! As the tram got nearer to Orford Place, a procession of bicycles and cars began to follow it and just before the last stop a chorus of *For he's a jolly good driver* was yelled by passengers and a collection made for him. At the tram sheds the crowd attempted to join hands for another burst of *Auld Lang Syne*, though this failed due to the rush to get the autographs of Mr. G. Hill, the driver and Mr. B. Fisher, the conductor.

No sooner had the journey been completed than work began on lifting the tram lines, clearing the way for the era of motorised public transport.

The last tram to run on this particular route passes through St. Benedict's Gate on the 27th July 1935. Behind the van is a remnant of the city wall which had a hinge pin embedded in it, where one of the old gates used to hang. This was destroyed along with most of the buildings shown in the photograph, during the Norwich Blitz in April 1942.

It's hardly surprising that the narrow and intense St. Stephens Street was redeveloped and widened in the early 1960s. It is shown in 1961, shortly before redevelopment began, and is hardly recognisble as the wide, busy street it is today. Plans to widen it had been shelved since 1931 though were revived after the rebuilding of the *Boar's Head* corner in 1953 and the Millet's corner five years later. By 1963, though the scheme was not fully completed for another year, the street was able to cope with two-way traffic after twenty-five years of being one-way. Provision was made for two seven-storey office blocks to be built, which were eventually erected in 1974 and 1977.

A view of the Gaumont Cinema, advertising its farewell show, shortly before its demolition in 1959. It opened in 1911 and was originally known as the 'Haymarket Picture House' but was renamed after it was purchased by the Gaumont Picture Company Corporation. Today the site is occupied by Top Shop. Among the other cinemas which have disappeared from the City's streets are the *Theatre de Luxe*, the *Electric*, the *Carlton*, the *Regal*, the *Ritz*, the *Thatched* and the *Mayfair*.

Situated at the bottom of Surrey Street, the *Boar's Head* was one of Norwich's best known inns. Originally believed to have been a private dwelling, one of its residents was Richard Browne, who was an Alderman of Norwich in 1456.

Despite thatched roofs being forbidden in the City in 1509 and in 1570, for some reason the *Boar's Head* was exempt from this rule along with a few other buildings. The inn's original name was the *Greyhound*, but it was renamed in the early 19th century after being bought by John Norgate, whose family crest had a boar's head on it. In 1926 radical restoration work was carried out on the ancient building though the thatched roof still remained. However all of this restoration work was in vain because on the night of April 27th 1942 the *Boar's Head* was gutted by firebombs during the same German air raid which devastated the area around Rampant Horse Street. Only a skeleton of the once picturesque inn remained, but a new *Boar's Head* rose on the same corner. In 1977 it became a branch of Lloyds Bank.

Castle Meadow from Davey Place circa 1910, showing three forms of early transport. In 1926 this narrow road was widened with the Castle losing a strip of its land as a result. Though not a single motor car is in sight, the disregard seemingly shown for fellow road users would not be out of place in the present day!

Castle Meadow forty years later in 1950. The road was widened in 1926 and for almost nine years the awkward tram tracks ran along close to the central islands. In 1935 the trams were withdrawn and replaced by buses and the era of the motor vehicle prevailed. Recently the large buses have been replaced on the routes within the City with smaller, more economical buses on the mini-line services.

Note the barrow belonging to the Norwich Window and Carpet Cleaning Company on the extreme right of the photograph, an example of a cheaper and cleaner, though more tiring, method of transport!

Looking down Westlegate from All Saints' Green; two pictures which show the changing skyline of Norwich. The first is from the mid-fifties and shows a public house called *The Tuns* on the left, which has since been 'improved' and renamed the *Pig and Whistle*. The Tudor-style building beyond the bare trees was also a pub, known as the *Barking Dickey*, which is now occupied by an investment information company.

This view shows the same area in the mid-sixties with Westlegate House (also known as the 'Glass Tower') now dominating the landscape.

Tram No. 25 travels down Gentleman's Walk, on Easter Sunday, 1915. Notice the muddle of overhead wires which were needed by trams and street lights.

William A. Clark, who had premises in Orford Hill, was a prominent ironmonger in the latter half of the nineteenth century. It is clear that the proprietor believed in advertising as every available wall space has been covered with lettering!

Before the building was demolished in 1898, the *Bell Hotel* had been built adjoining the premises.

Today it would be considered unthinkable, but cattle were frequently herded through the streets of the City from the cattle market. Here we see the cattle being driven through Charing Cross and St Andrews Hill, en route to Midland Station from the market.